Trace each dotted line from the child to the ice cream.

Curriculum Area: Language Arts **Skills:** Left-to-Right Tracing, Pre-Writing, Fine Motor Skills

Trace each dotted line from the worm to the apple.

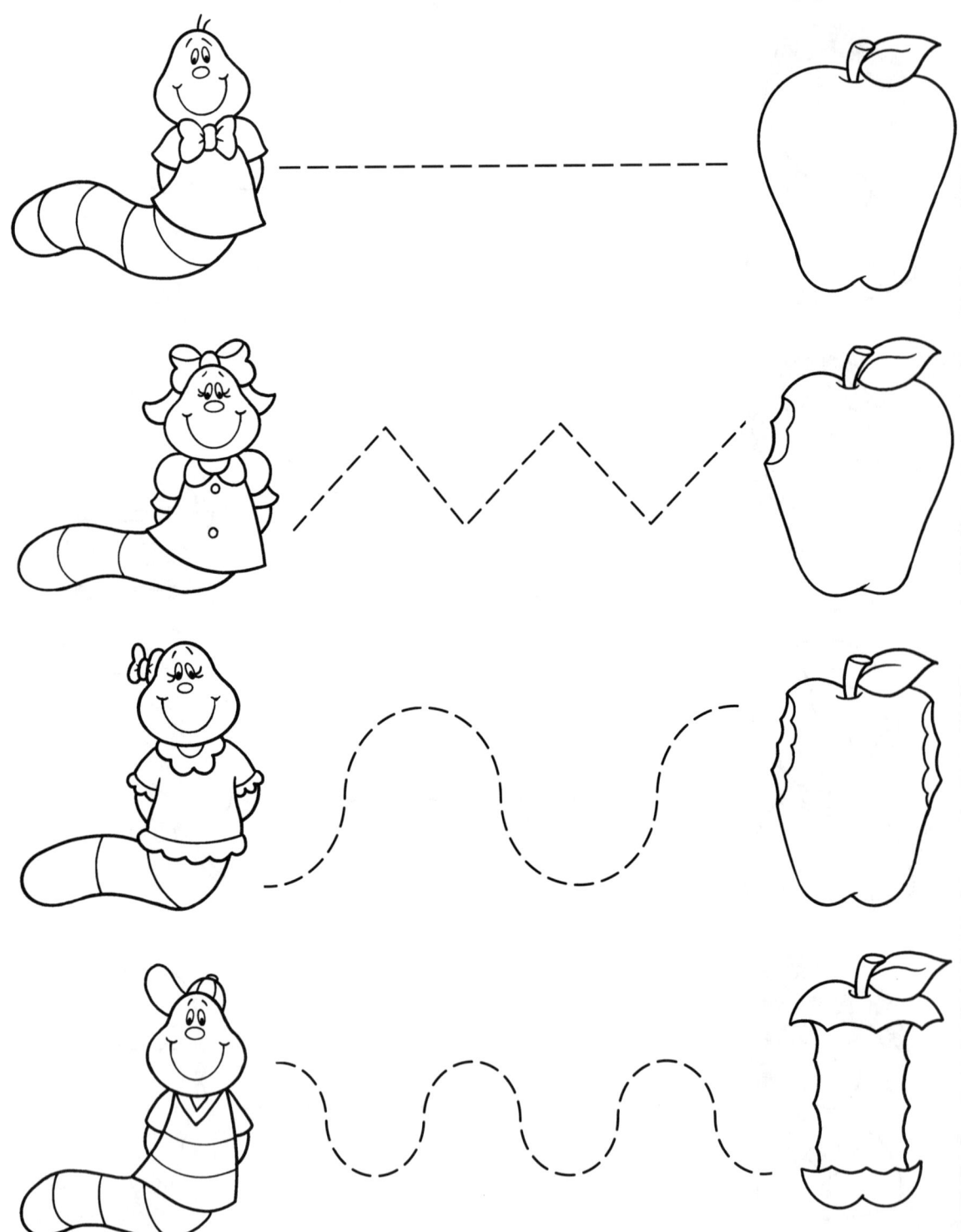

Curriculum Area: Language Arts **Skills:** Left-to-Right Tracing, Pre-Writing, Fine Motor Skills

Follow the path from each bird to its nest.

Curriculum Area: Language Arts   **Skills:** Following a Path, Pre-Writing, Fine Motor Skills

Follow the path from each dog to its house.

Curriculum Area: Language Arts **Skills:** Following a Path, Pre-Writing, Fine Motor Skills

Follow the path from the clown to his car.

Curriculum Area: Language Arts   **Skills:** Following a Path, Pre-Writing, Fine Motor Skills

Follow the path from the cow to the barn.

Curriculum Area: Language Arts **Skills:** Following a Path, Pre-Writing, Fine Motor Skills

Follow the path from the frog to the lily pad.

Curriculum Area: Language Arts   **Skills:** Following a Path, Pre-Writing, Fine Motor Skills

Follow the path from the squirrel to the acorn.

Curriculum Area: Language Arts   **Skills:** Following a Path, Pre-Writing, Fine Motor Skills

Trace the flowers and leaves. **Color** the picture.

Trace the wings of each butterfly. **Color** the picture.

Trace each star. **Color** the picture.

Curriculum Area: Language Arts **Skills:** Tracing, Coloring, Pre-Writing, Fine Motor Skills

Draw a line between the matching objects.

Curriculum Area: Language Arts   **Skills:** Matching, Pre-Writing, Fine Motor Skills

Draw a line between the **matching** objects.

Curriculum Area: Language Arts   **Skills:** Matching, Pre-Writing, Fine Motor Skills

Draw a circle around each **food**. Put an X on each **toy**.

Draw a circle around each **animal**. Put an X on each **flower**.

Draw a line from each **big** item to the matching **small** item.

Draw a line from each **small** item to the matching **big** item.

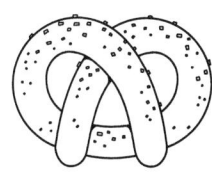

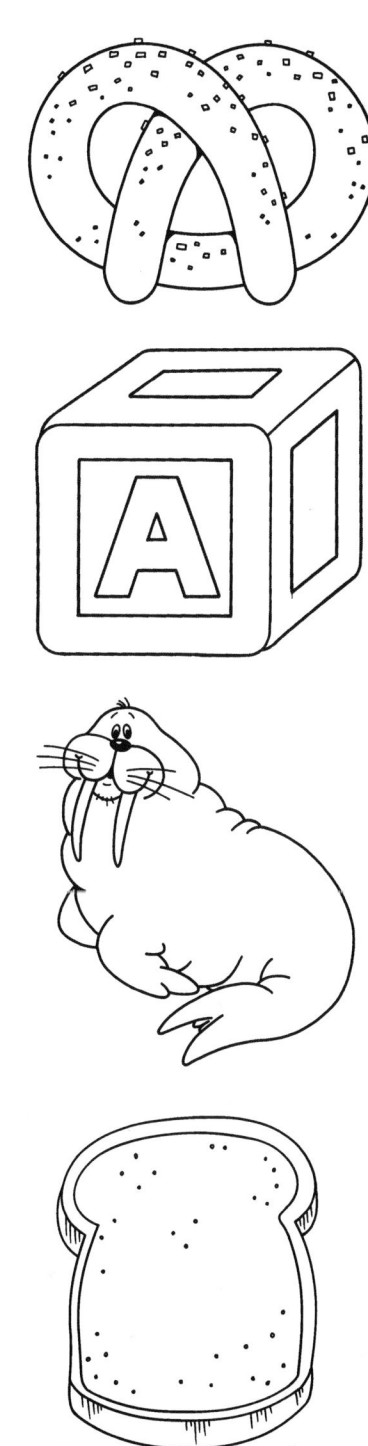

Curriculum Area: Language Arts   **Skills:** Differentiating between Big and Small, Matching

In each row, circle the **matching** pictures.

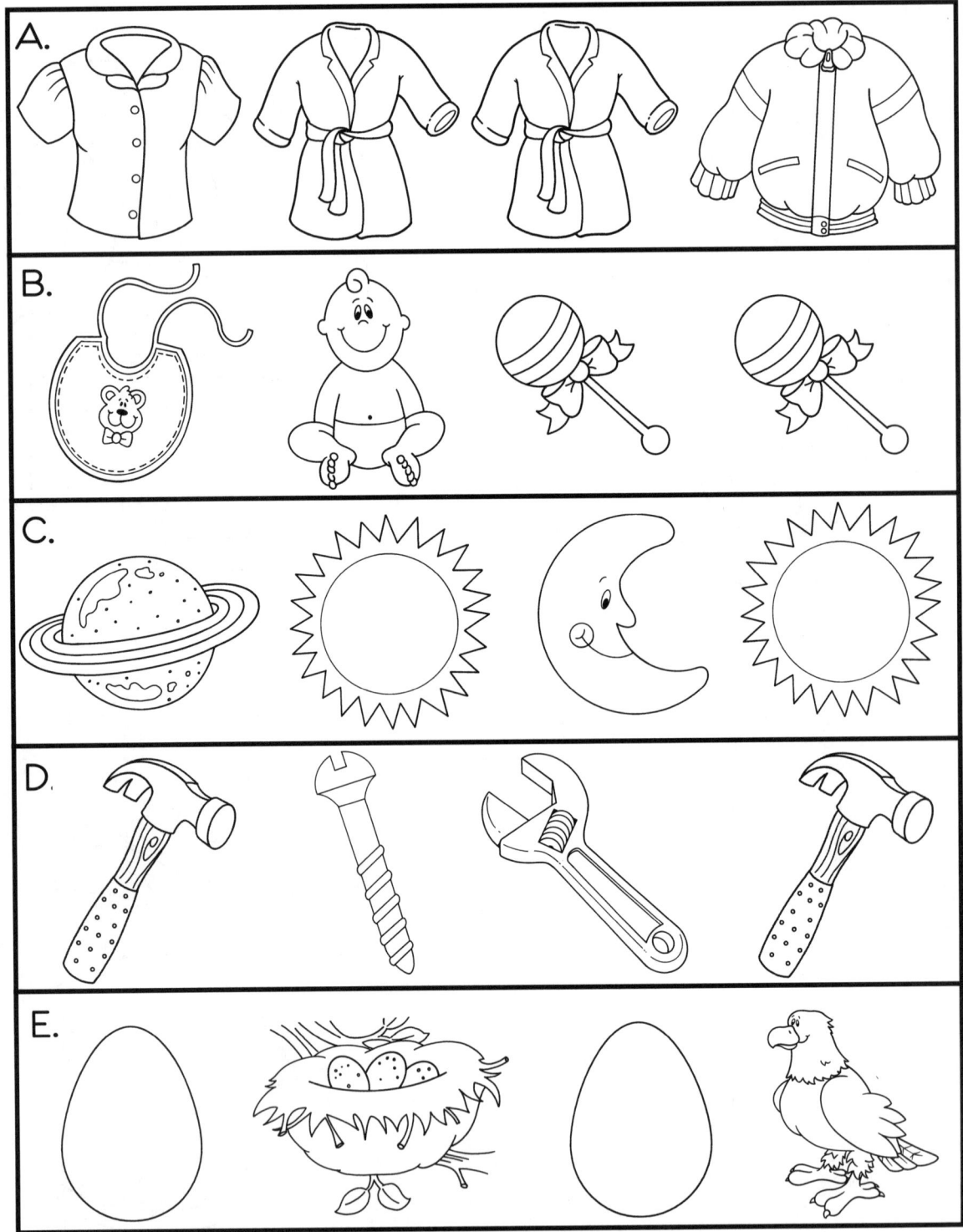

In each row, put an X on the picture that is **different**.

Curriculum Area: Language Arts   **Skills:** Visual Discrimination, Pre-Writing, Fine Motor Skills

Draw a line between the **objects that belong together**.

Curriculum Area: Language Arts **Skills:** Pairing, Pre-Writing, Fine Motor Skills

Trace each shape. Say the name of each shape as you trace it. Color each shape.

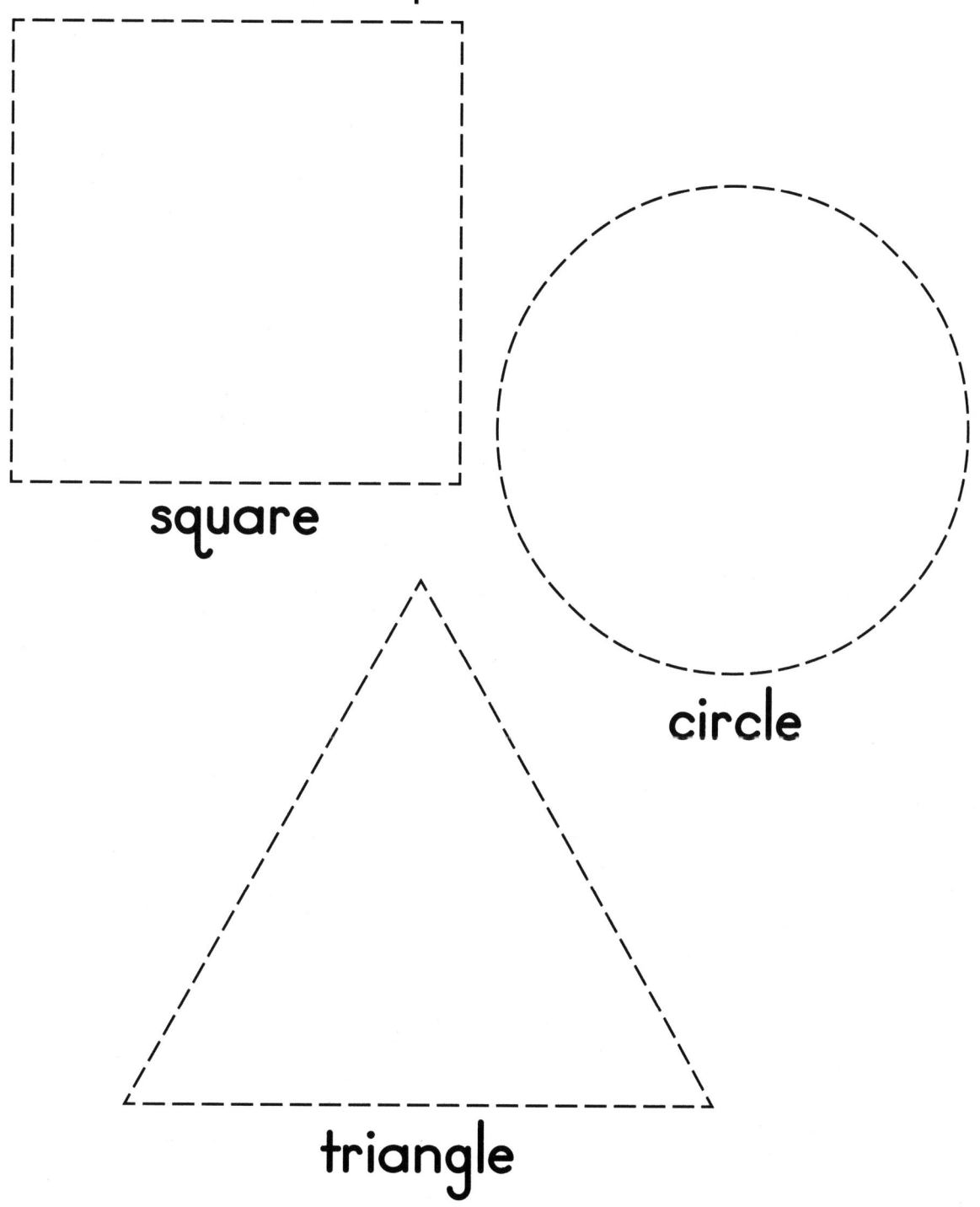

Trace each shape. Say the name of each shape as you trace it. Color each shape.

rectangle

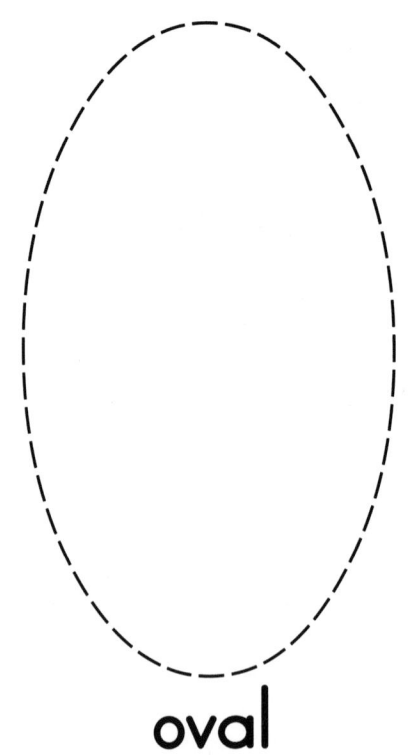

oval

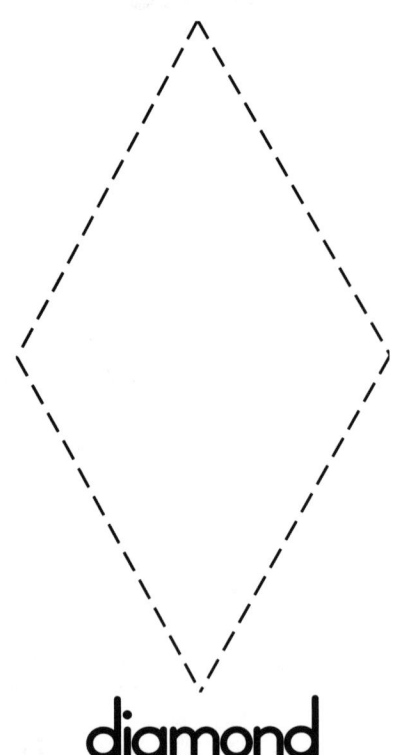

diamond

Curriculum Area: Math   **Skills:** Recognizing Shapes, Tracing, Pre-Writing

Trace each **shape**. Say the name of each shape as you trace it. Color each shape.

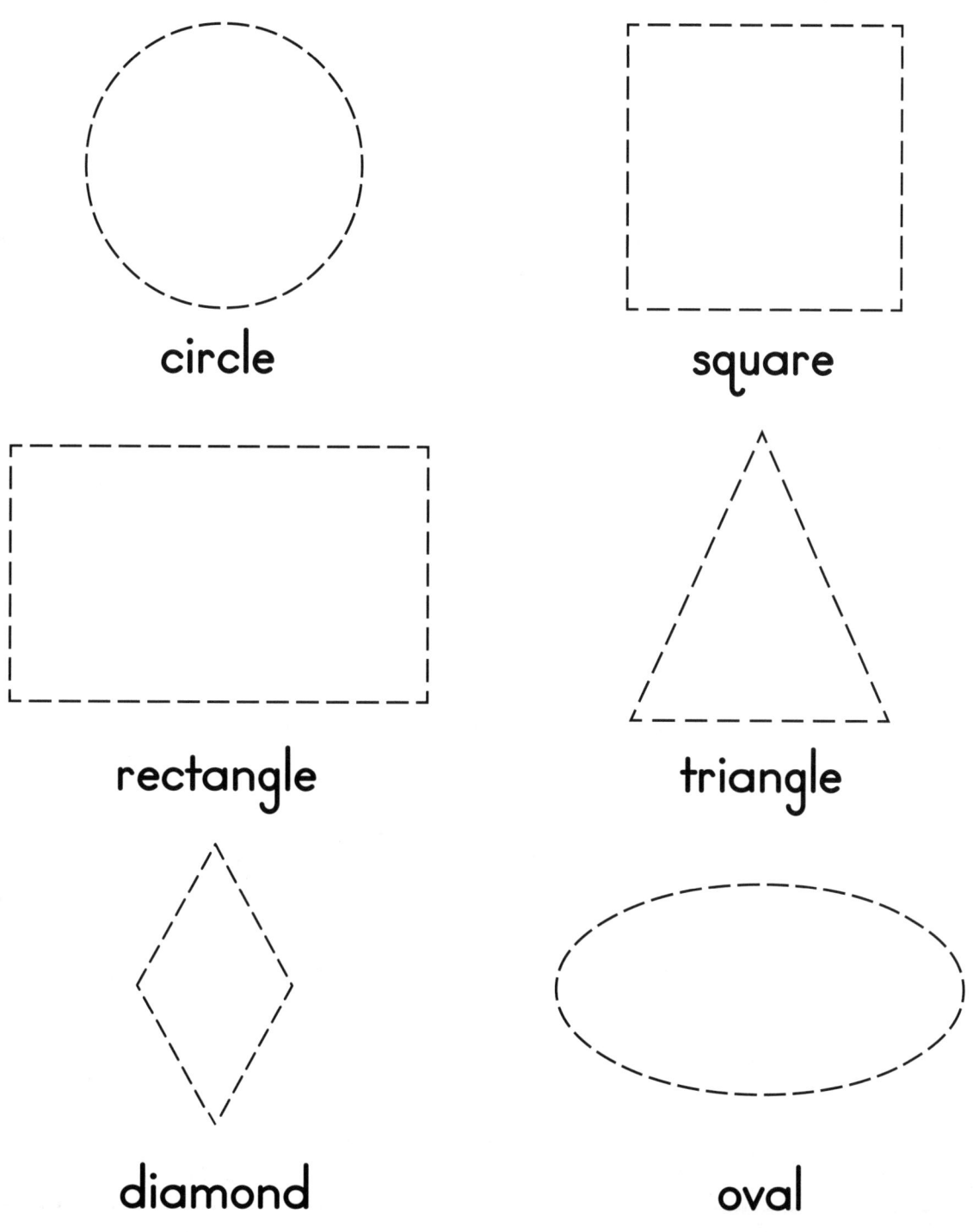

Look at the first shape in each row. Color the shape in the row that is the **same**.

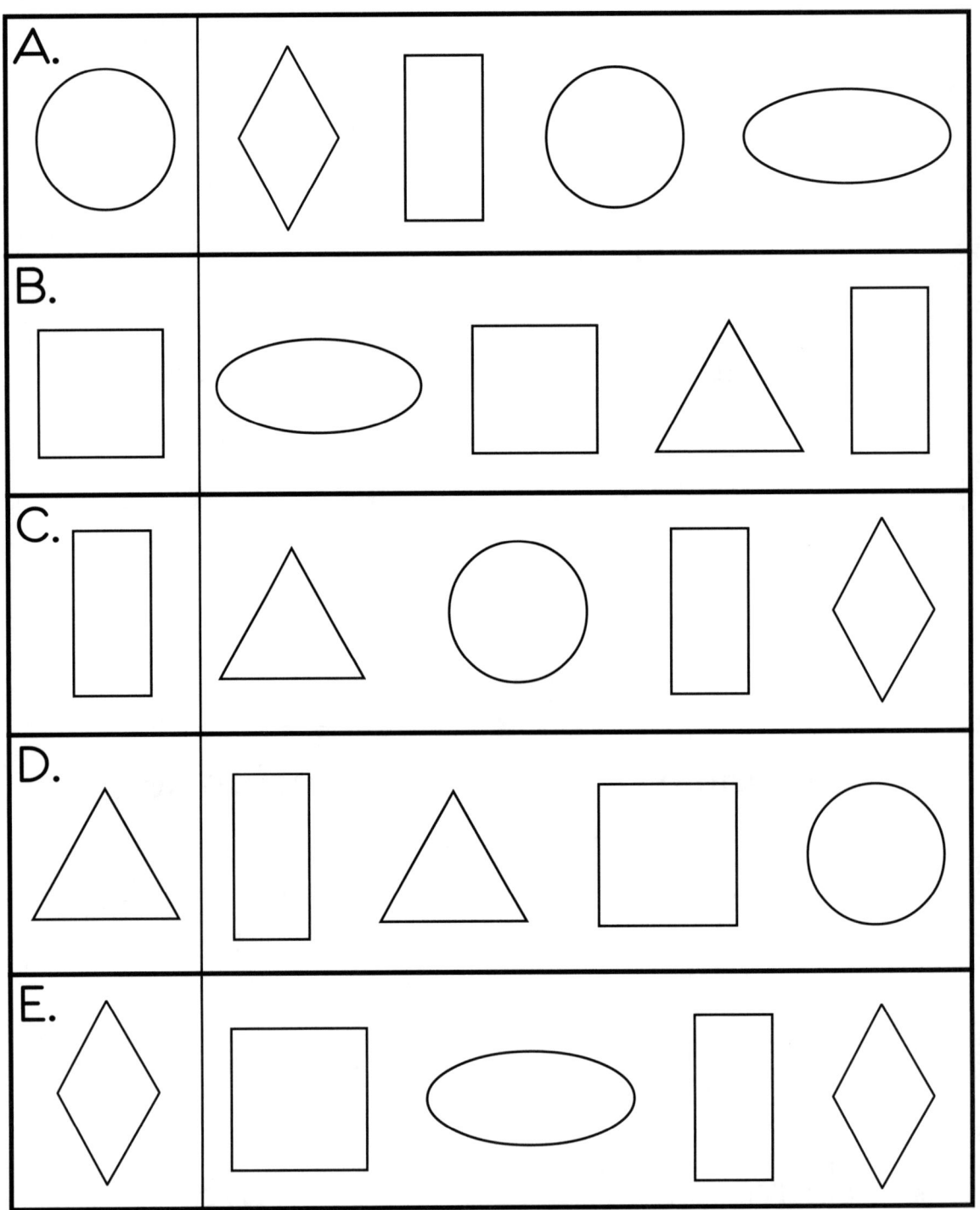

Color the shape in each row that is **different**.

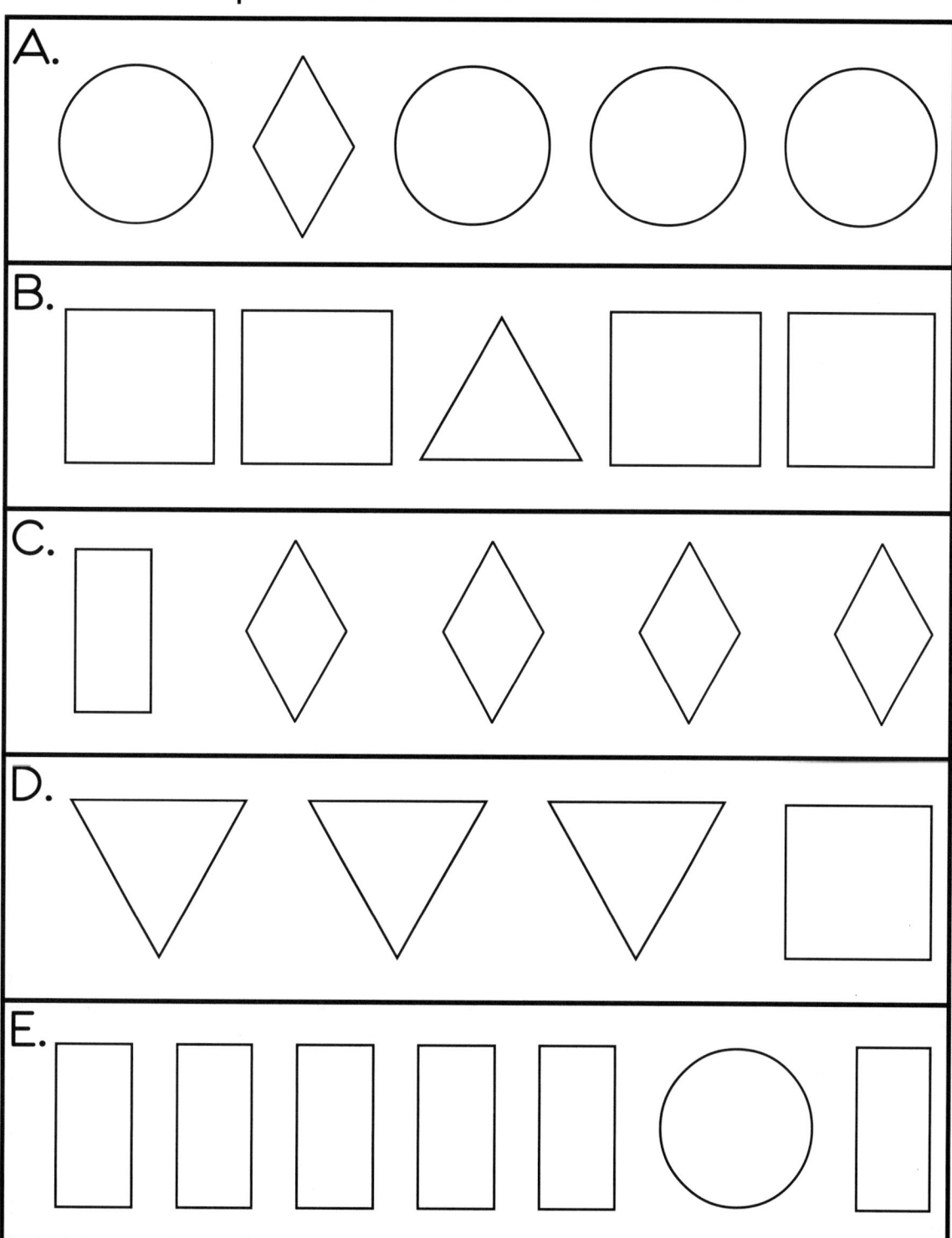

Curriculum Area: Math   **Skills:** Recognizing Shapes, Visual Discrimination, Coloring

Look at the **pattern** in each row. Fill in the blank with the shape that comes next.

A. circle, square, circle, square, ___

B. triangle, circle, triangle, circle, ___

C. diamond, rectangle, diamond, rectangle, ___

D. rectangle, triangle, rectangle, triangle, ___

E. square, oval, square, oval, ___

Curriculum Area: Math   **Skills:** Patterning, Recognizing Shapes, Drawing

Look at the **pattern** in each row. Fill in the blank with the shape that comes next.

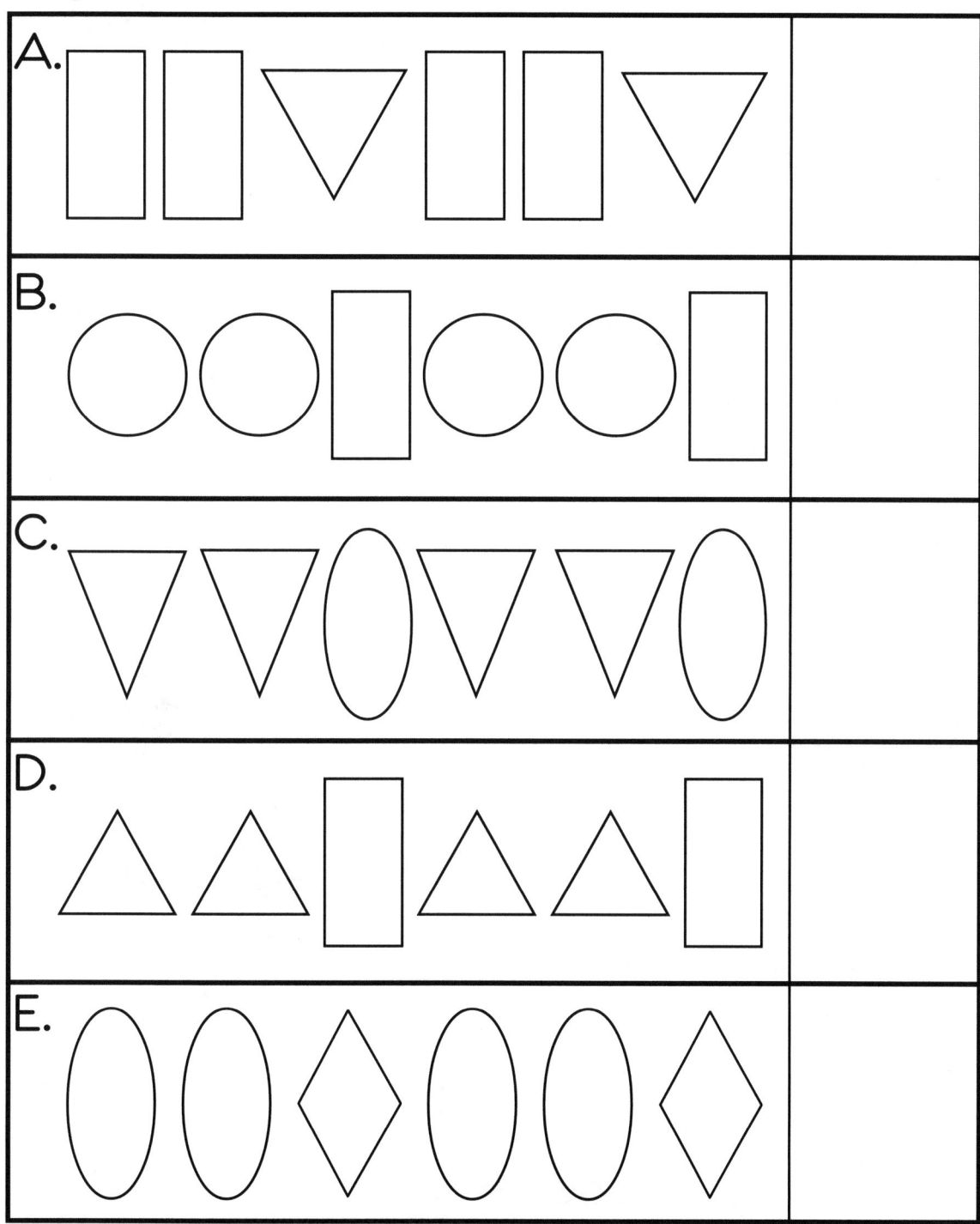

Curriculum Area: Math   **Skills:** Patterning, Recognizing Shapes, Drawing

Color all of the items **red**. Say the name of each item as you color it.

Color all of the items **blue**. Say the name of each item as you color it.

blue jay

blueberries

crayon

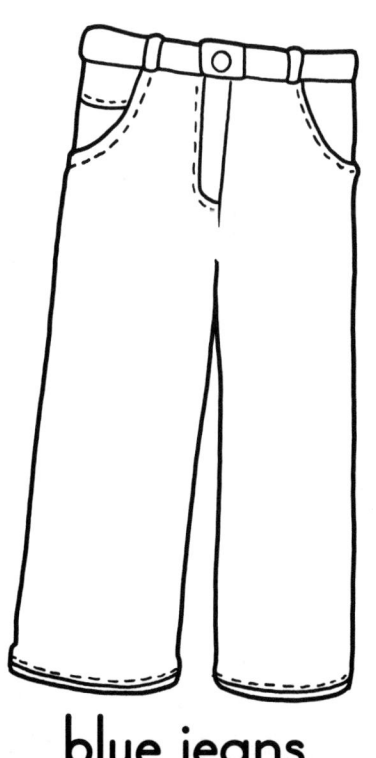

morning glories

blue jeans

Curriculum Area: Language Arts   **Skills:** Recognizing Colors, Identifying Objects, Fine Motor Skills

Color all of the items **green**. Say the name of each item as you color it.

cactus

frog

grass

turtle

pine tree

Curriculum Area: Language Arts **Skills:** Recognizing Colors, Identifying Objects, Fine Motor Skills

Pull-Out Answer Key

Page 1
Each dotted line should be traced from the child to the ice cream.

Page 2
Each dotted line should be traced from the worm to the apple.

Page 3
Each path should be followed from the bird to its nest.

Page 4
Each path should be followed from the dog to its house.

Page 5
The path should be followed from the clown to the car.

Page 6
The path should be followed from the cow to the barn.

Page 7
The path should be followed from the frog to the lily pad.

Page 8
The path should be followed from the squirrel to the acorn.

Page 9
The flowers and leaves should be traced and colored.

Page 10
The wings of each butterfly should be traced and the butterflies colored.

Page 11
The stars should all be traced and the picture colored.

Page 12
A line should be drawn between each pair of matching objects.

Page 13
A line should be drawn between each pair of matching objects.

Page 14
The following should be circled: apple, cake, sandwich
The following should be marked with an X: bicycle, doll, yo-yo

Page 15
The following should be circled: gorilla, butterfly, giraffe
The following should be marked with an X: the three flower blossoms

Page 16
A line should be drawn between each big item and its smaller match.

Page 17
A line should be drawn between each small item and its bigger match.

Page 18
The following should be circled:
A. two robes
B. two rattles
C. two suns
D. two hammers
E. two eggs

Page 19
The following should be marked with an X:
A. car without wheels
B. dog without spots
C. girl with bow
D. pie missing a slice
E. open book

Page 20
A line should be drawn between the following:

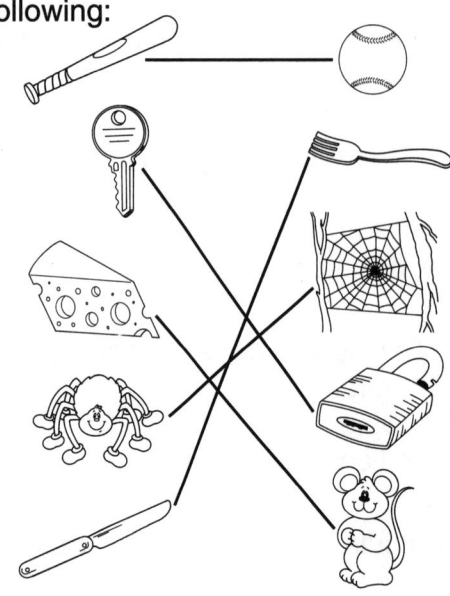

Page 21
Each shape should be traced and colored.

Page 22
Each shape should be traced and colored.

Page 23
Each shape should be traced and colored.

Page 24
The following shapes should be colored:
A. circle
B. square
C. rectangle
D. triangle
E. diamond

Page 25
The following shapes should be colored:
A. diamond
B. triangle
C. rectangle
D. square
E. circle

Page 26
The next shape in the pattern should be:
A. circle
B. triangle
C. diamond
D. rectangle
E. square

Page 27
The next shape in the pattern should be:
A. rectangle
B. circle
C. triangle
D. triangle
E. oval

Page 28
All items should be colored red.

Page 29
All items should be colored blue.

Page 30
All items should be colored green.

Page 31
All items should be colored yellow.

Page 32
All items should be colored purple.

Page 33
All items should be colored orange.

Page 34
All items should be colored black.

Page 35
All items should be colored brown.

Page 36
All items should be colored white.

Page 37
Items should be colored and matched as shown:

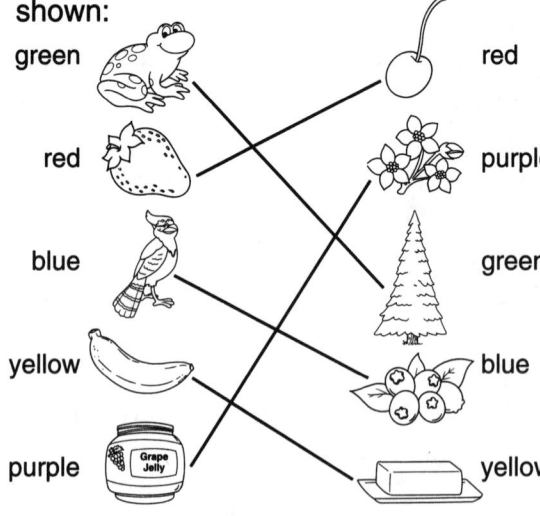

Page 38
Items should be colored and matched as shown:

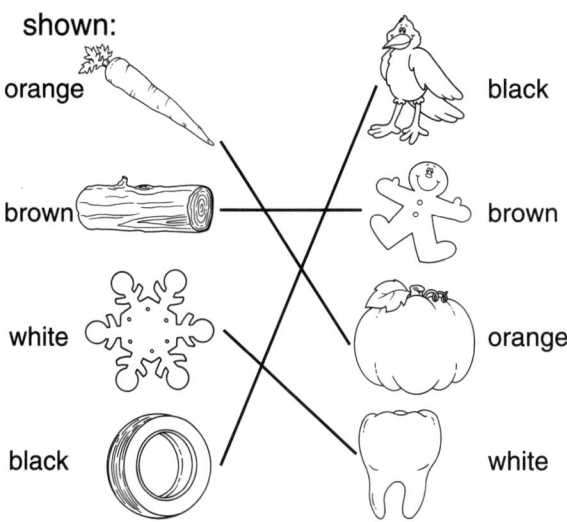

Pages 39–51
The shaded letters on each page should be traced.
The blank lines should then be used to practice printing the letters.

Page 52
In each box, the larger of the two items should be colored blue.
In each box, the smaller of the two items should be colored red.

Page 53
In each row, the tall clown should be colored green.
In each row, the medium clown should be colored purple.
In each row, the short clown should be colored orange.

Page 54
The sets should be matched as shown:

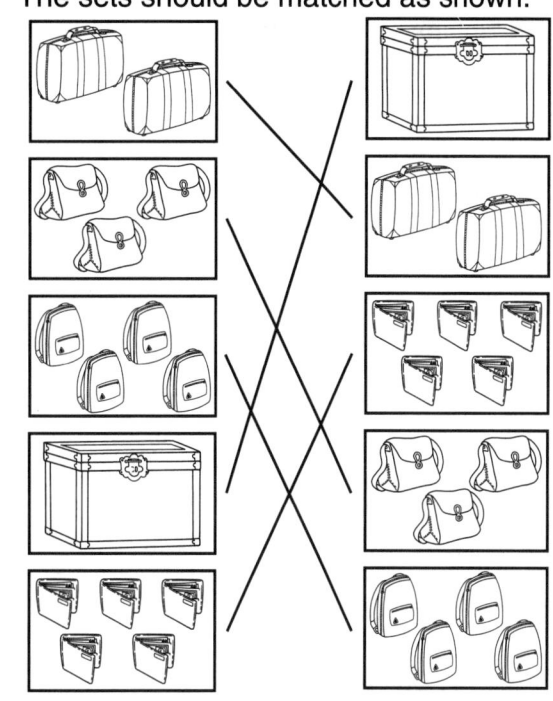

Page 55
The sets should be matched as shown:

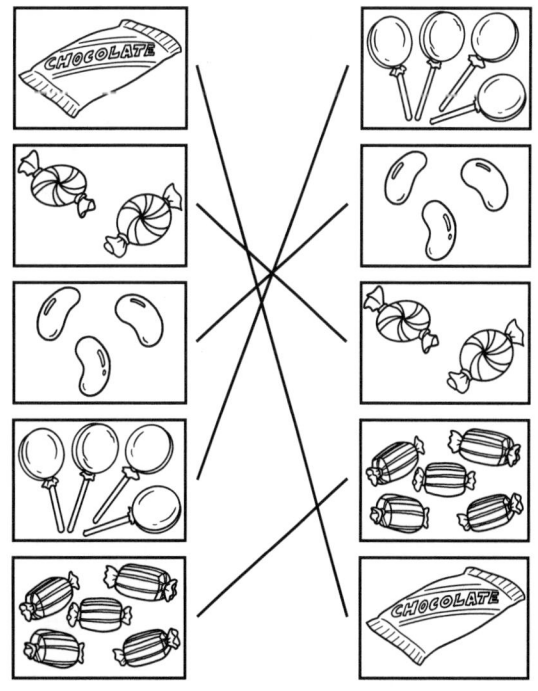

Page 56
Each shaded numeral should be traced. The blank lines should then be used to practice printing the numerals.

Page 57
The numerals should be matched to the sets as shown:

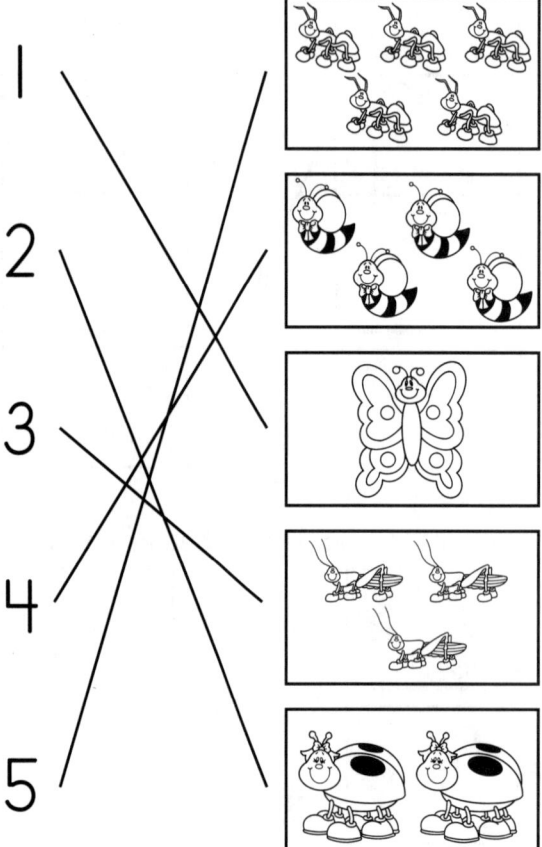

Page 58
The numerals should be matched to the sets as shown:

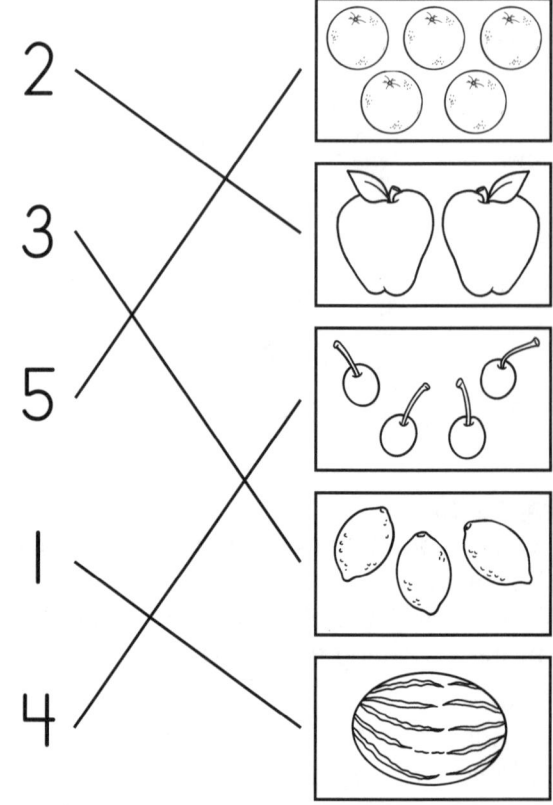

Page 59
The following toys should be circled:
A. one yo-yo
B. two skates
C. three dolls
D. four drums
E. five jacks

Page 60
The following animals should be circled:
A. four lions
B. one mouse
C. two sheep
D. five penguins
E. three koala bears

Color all of the items **yellow**. Say the name of each item as you color it.

butter

chick

sunflower

star

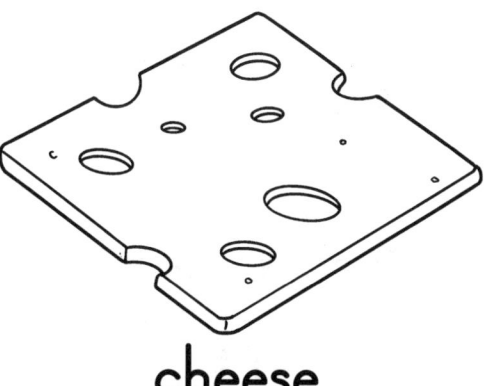

cheese

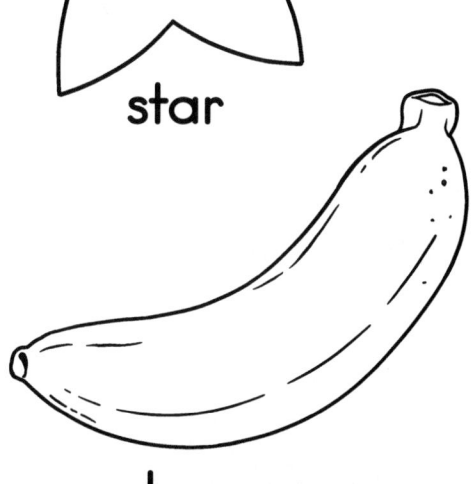

banana

Curriculum Area: Language Arts   **Skills:** Recognizing Colors, Identifying Objects, Fine Motor Skills

Color all of the items **purple**. Say the name of each item as you color it.

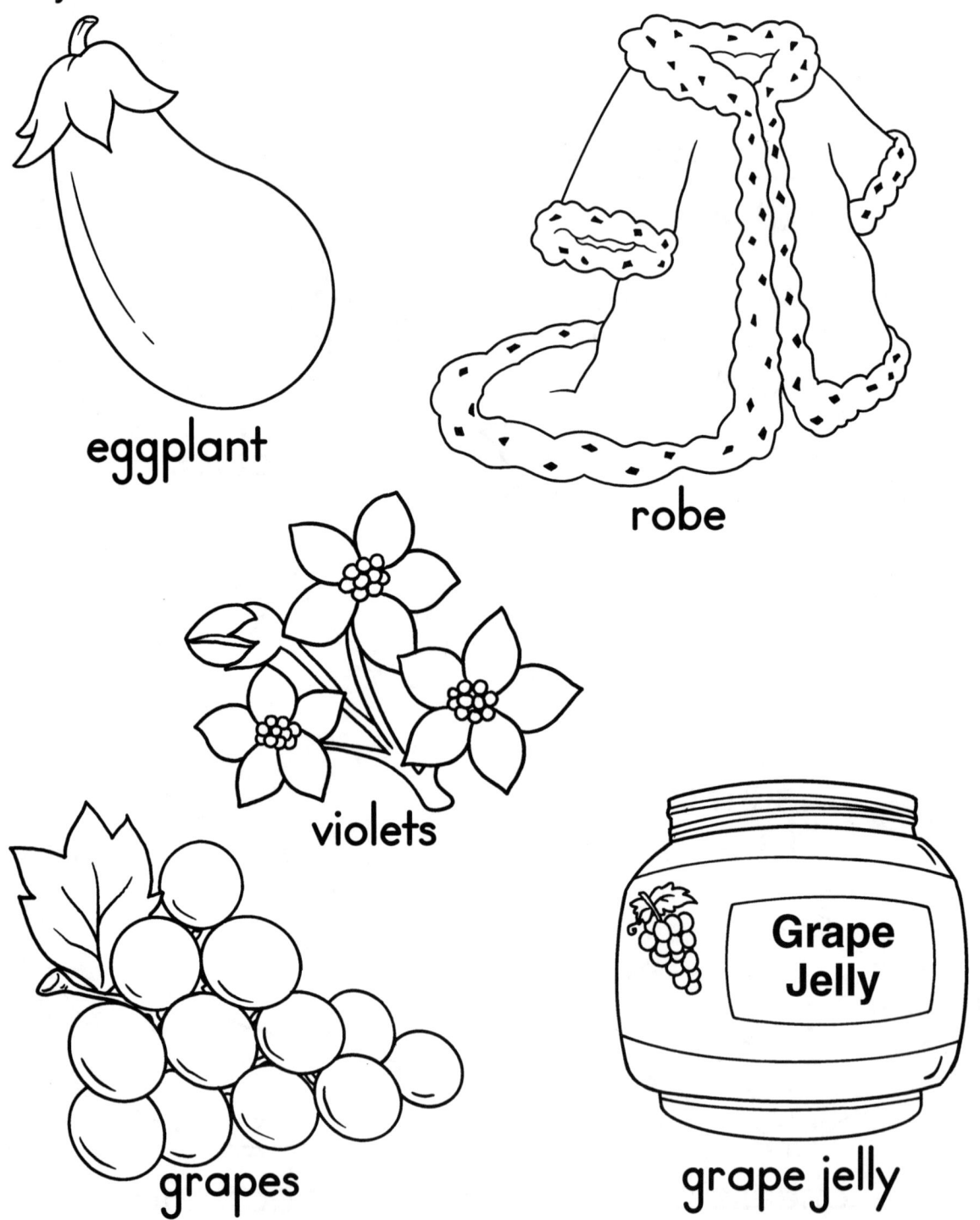

Color all of the items **orange**. Say the name of each item as you color it.

orange

leaf

carrot

pumpkin

basketball

Curriculum Area: Language Arts   **Skills:** Recognizing Colors, Identifying Objects, Fine Motor Skills

Color all of the items **black**. Say the name of each item as you color it.

spider

bat

coal

tire

crow

Curriculum Area: Language Arts   **Skills:** Recognizing Colors, Identifying Objects, Fine Motor Skills

Color all of the items **brown**. Say the name of each item as you color it.

gingerbread man

bear

rabbit

log

bread

Curriculum Area: Language Arts   **Skills:** Recognizing Colors, Identifying Objects, Fine Motor Skills

Color all of the items **white**. Say the name of each item as you color it.

cloud

tooth

baseball

milk

snowman

snowflake

Curriculum Area: Language Arts **Skills:** Recognizing Colors, Identifying Objects, Fine Motor Skills

Color each item the correct color. Draw a line between the items that are the **same color**.

Color each item the correct color. Draw lines between the items that are the **same color**.

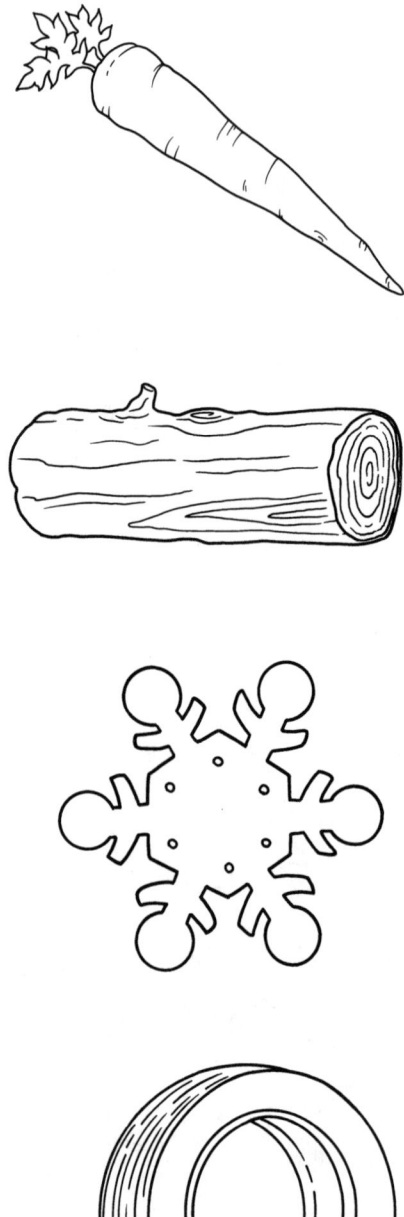

Trace and name each letter. **Practice printing** each letter on the blank lines.

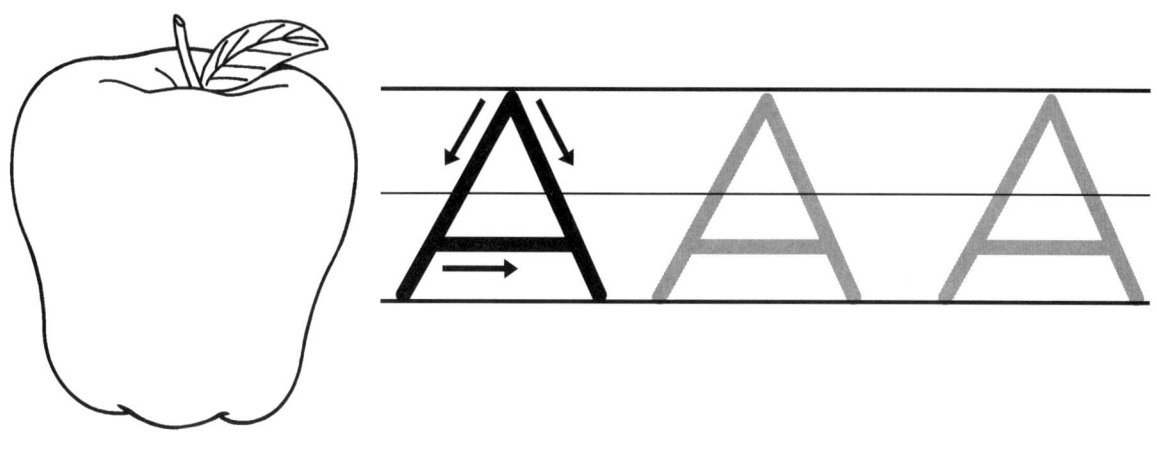

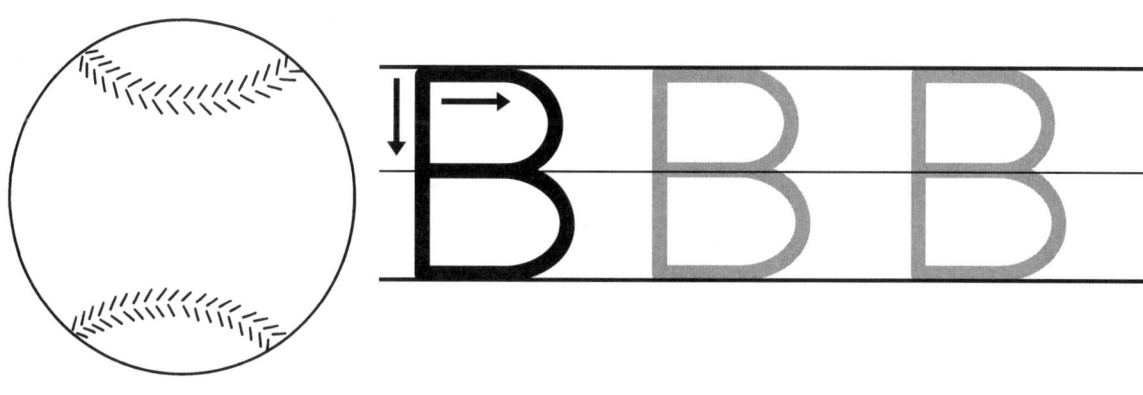

Curriculum Area: Language Arts   **Skills:** Recognizing Letters, Tracing, Printing

Trace and name each letter. **Practice printing** each letter on the blank lines.

Trace and name each letter. **Practice printing** each letter on the blank lines.

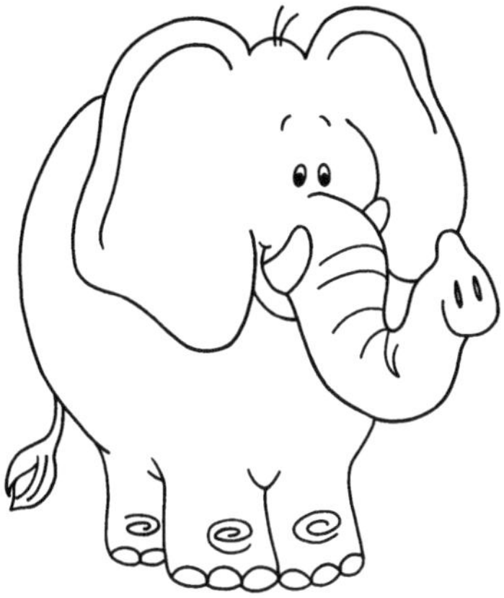

E E E

F F F

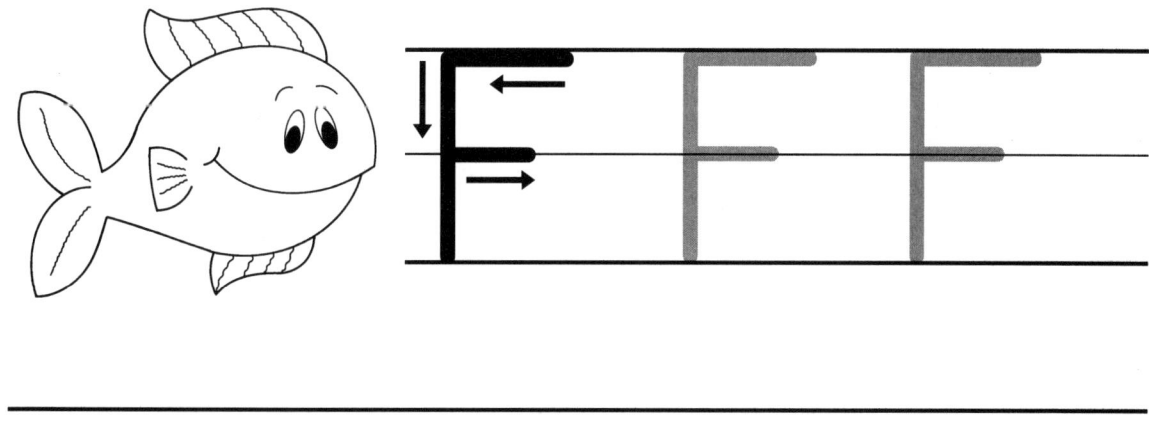

Curriculum Area: Language Arts **Skills:** Recognizing Letters, Tracing, Printing

Trace and name each letter. **Practice printing** each letter on the blank lines.

Trace and name each letter. **Practice printing** each letter on the blank lines.

Trace and name each letter. **Practice printing** each letter on the blank lines.

Curriculum Area: Language Arts **Skills:** Recognizing Letters, Tracing, Printing

Trace and name each letter. **Practice printing** each letter on the blank lines.

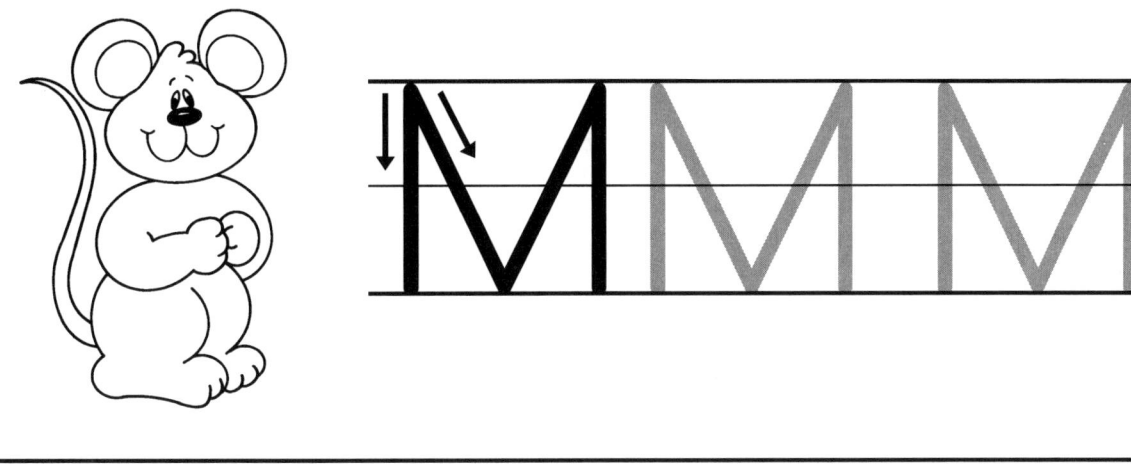

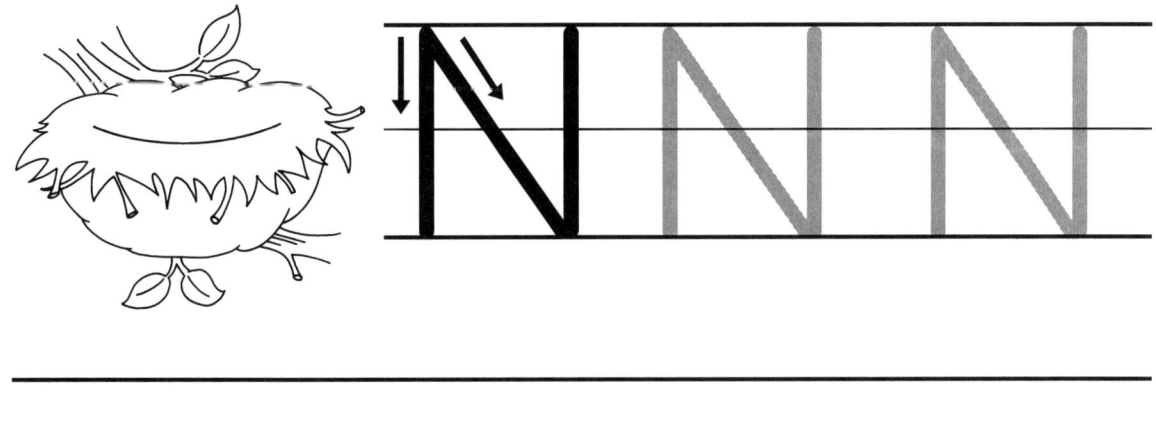

Curriculum Area: Language Arts **Skills:** Recognizing Letters, Tracing, Printing

Trace and name each letter. **Practice printing** each letter on the blank lines.

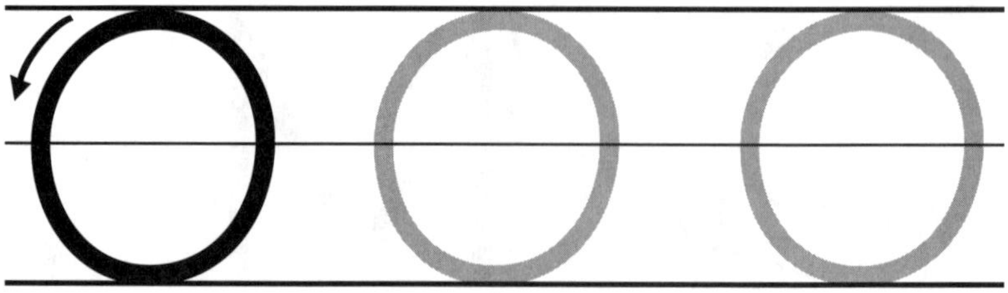

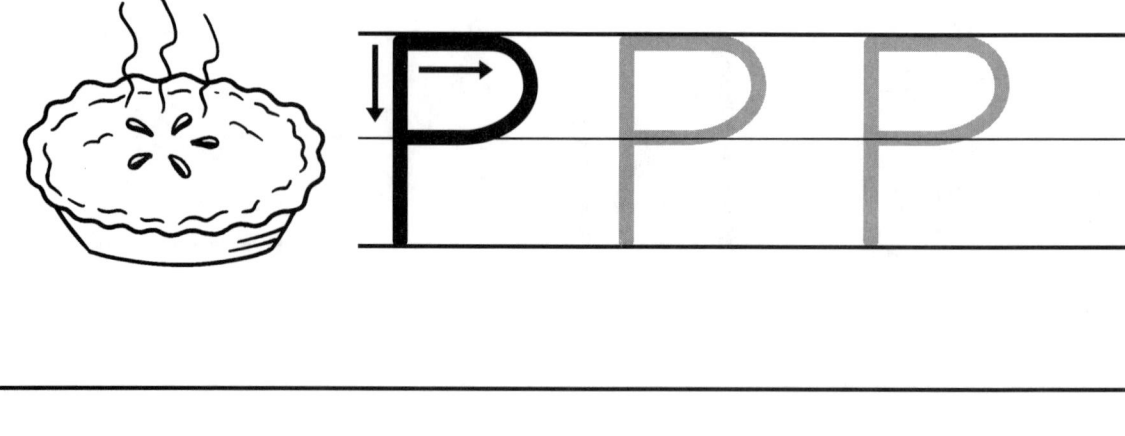

Curriculum Area: Language Arts **Skills:** Recognizing Letters, Tracing, Printing

Trace and name each letter. **Practice printing** each letter on the blank lines.

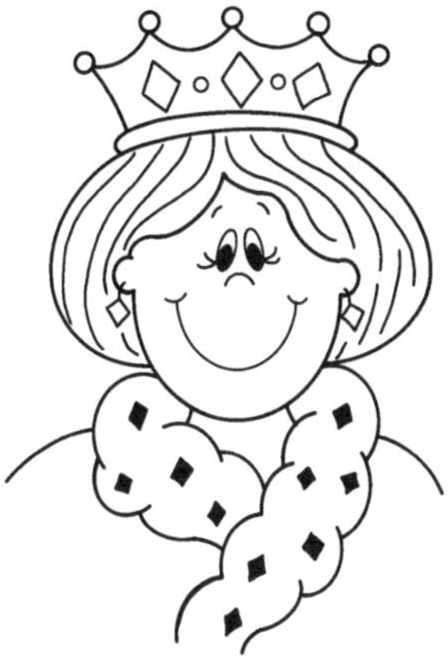

Q Q Q

R R R

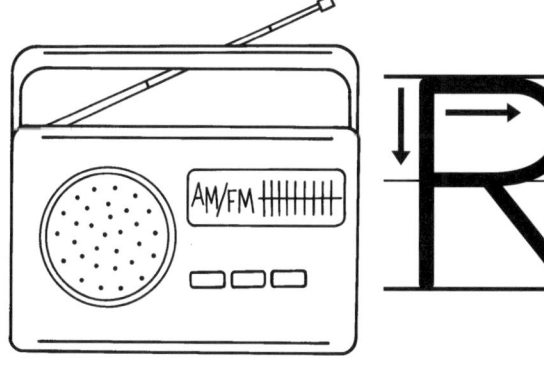

Curriculum Area: Language Arts **Skills:** Recognizing Letters, Tracing, Printing

Trace and name each letter. **Practice printing** each letter on the blank lines.

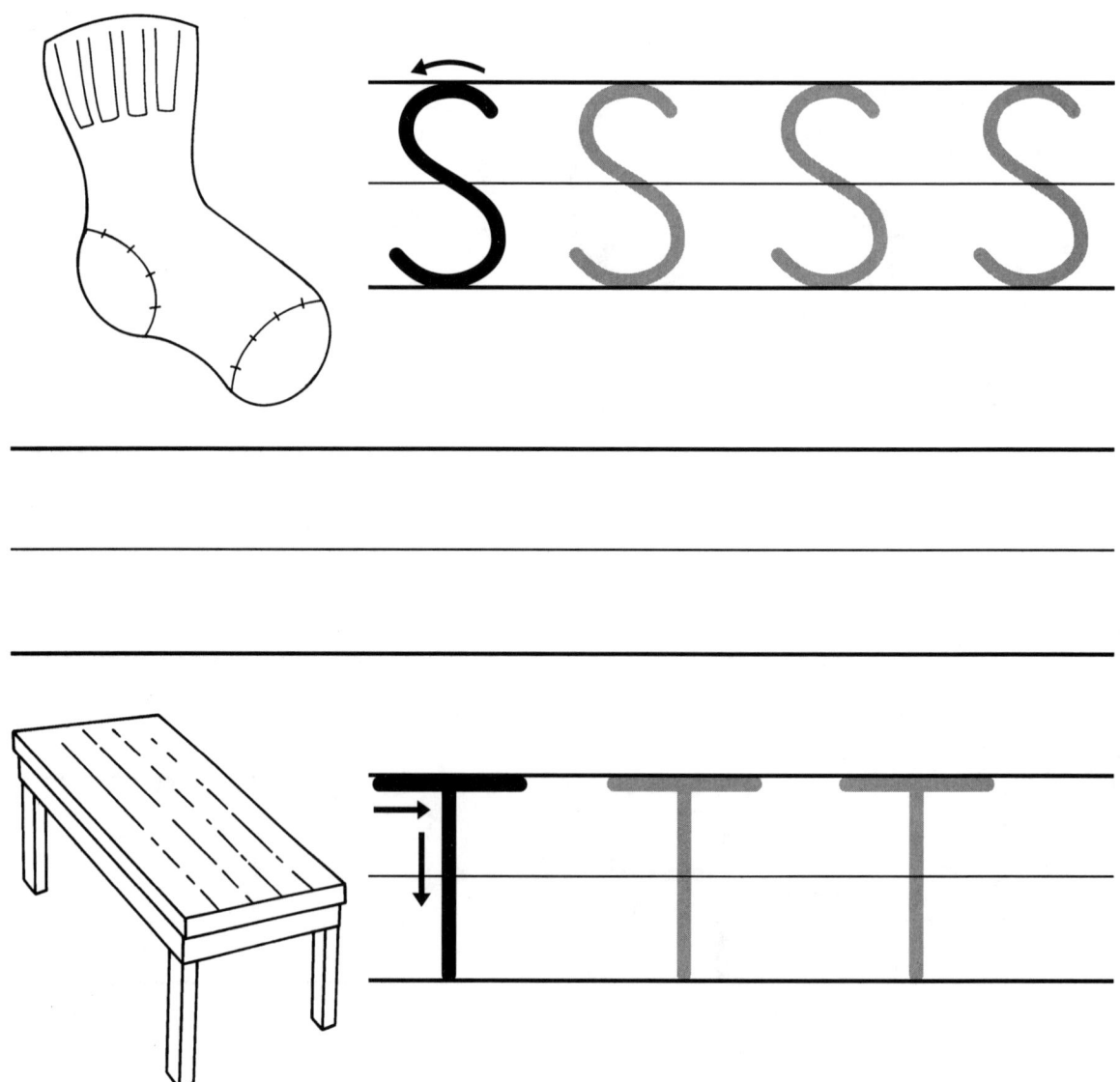

Trace and name each letter. **Practice printing** each letter on the blank lines.

Trace and name each letter. **Practice printing** each letter on the blank lines.

Trace and name each letter. **Practice printing** each letter on the blank lines.

In each box, color the **large** object blue.
In each box, color the **small** object red.

Curriculum Area: Language Arts **Skills:** Discriminating Between Sizes, Coloring, Pre-Writing

In each row, color the **tall** clown green. Color the **medium-sized** clown purple. Color the **short** clown orange.

A.

B.

Curriculum Area: Language Arts   **Skills:** Discriminating Between Sizes, Coloring, Pre-Writing

Draw a line between each **matching** set.

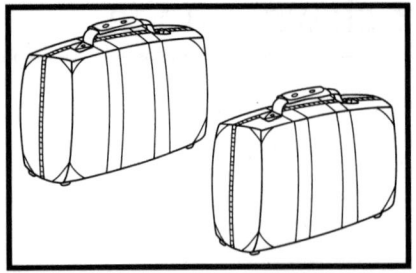
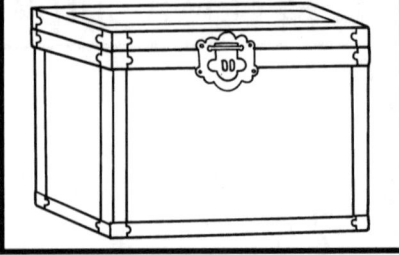
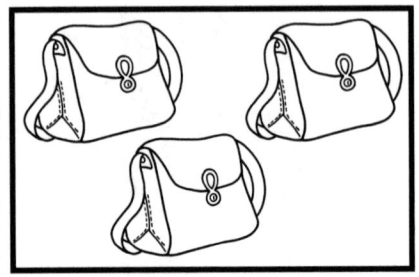
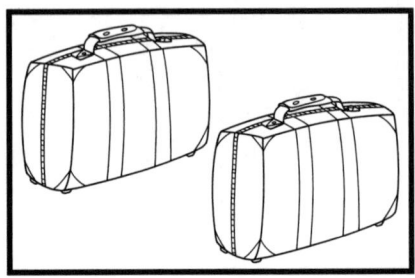
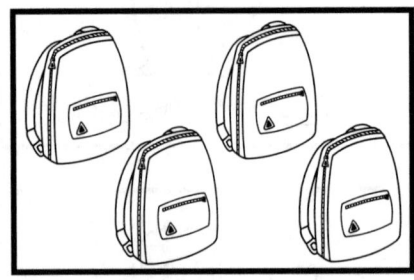
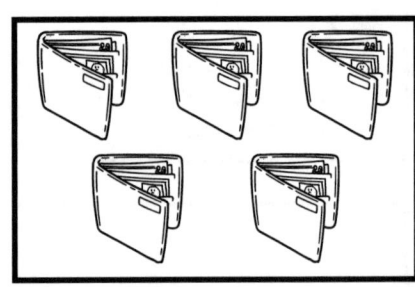
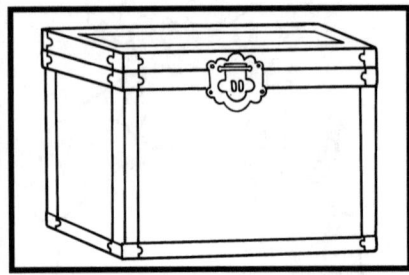
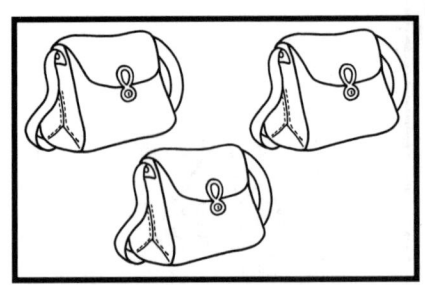
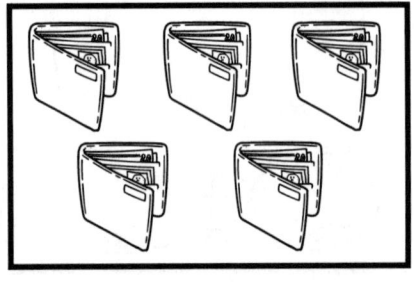
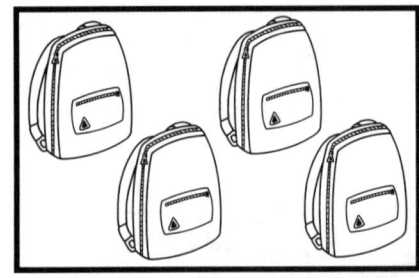

Curriculum Area: Math   **Skills:** Matching Sets, Counting, Fine Motor Skills

Draw a line between each **matching** set.

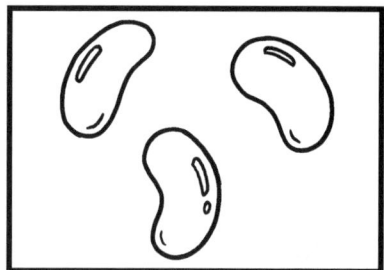

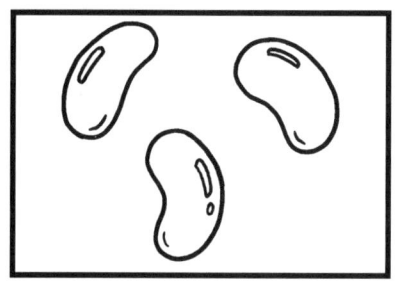

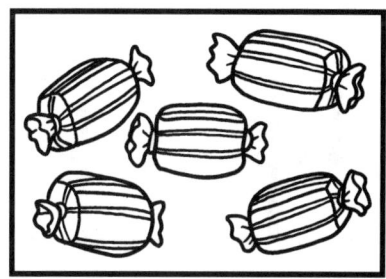

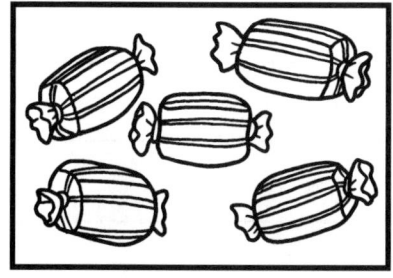

Curriculum Area: Math   **Skills:** Matching Sets, Counting, Fine Motor Skills

Trace and name each numeral. **Practice printing** the numeral in the blank space provided.

Curriculum Area: Math **Skills:** Identifying Numerals, Tracing, Printing, Fine Motor Skills

Draw a line to **match** each numeral to the correct set.

1

2

3

4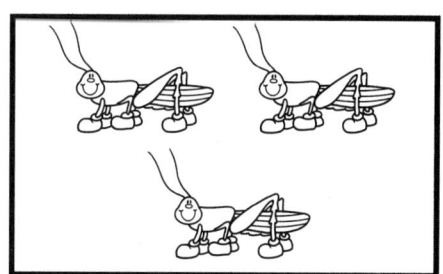

5

Curriculum Area: Math **Skills:** Matching Numerals to Sets, Counting

Draw a line to **match** each numeral to the correct set.

2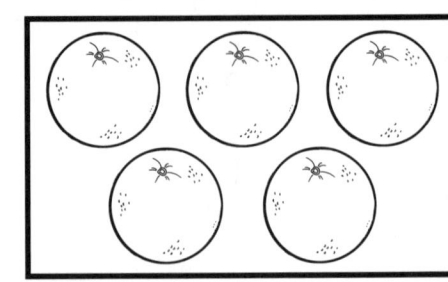

3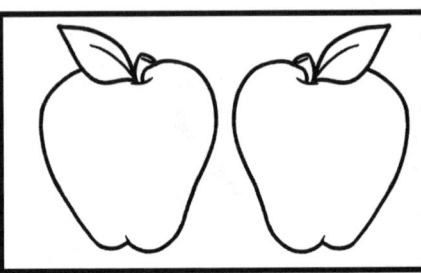

5

1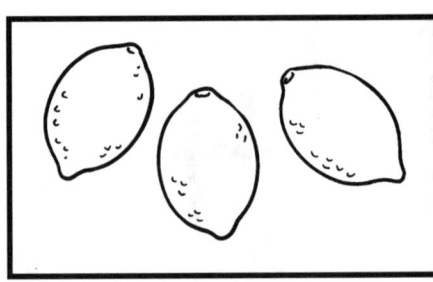

4

Curriculum Area: Math   **Skills:** Matching Numerals to Sets, Counting

Read the **numeral** at the beginning of each row. Put an X on that number of objects in the row.

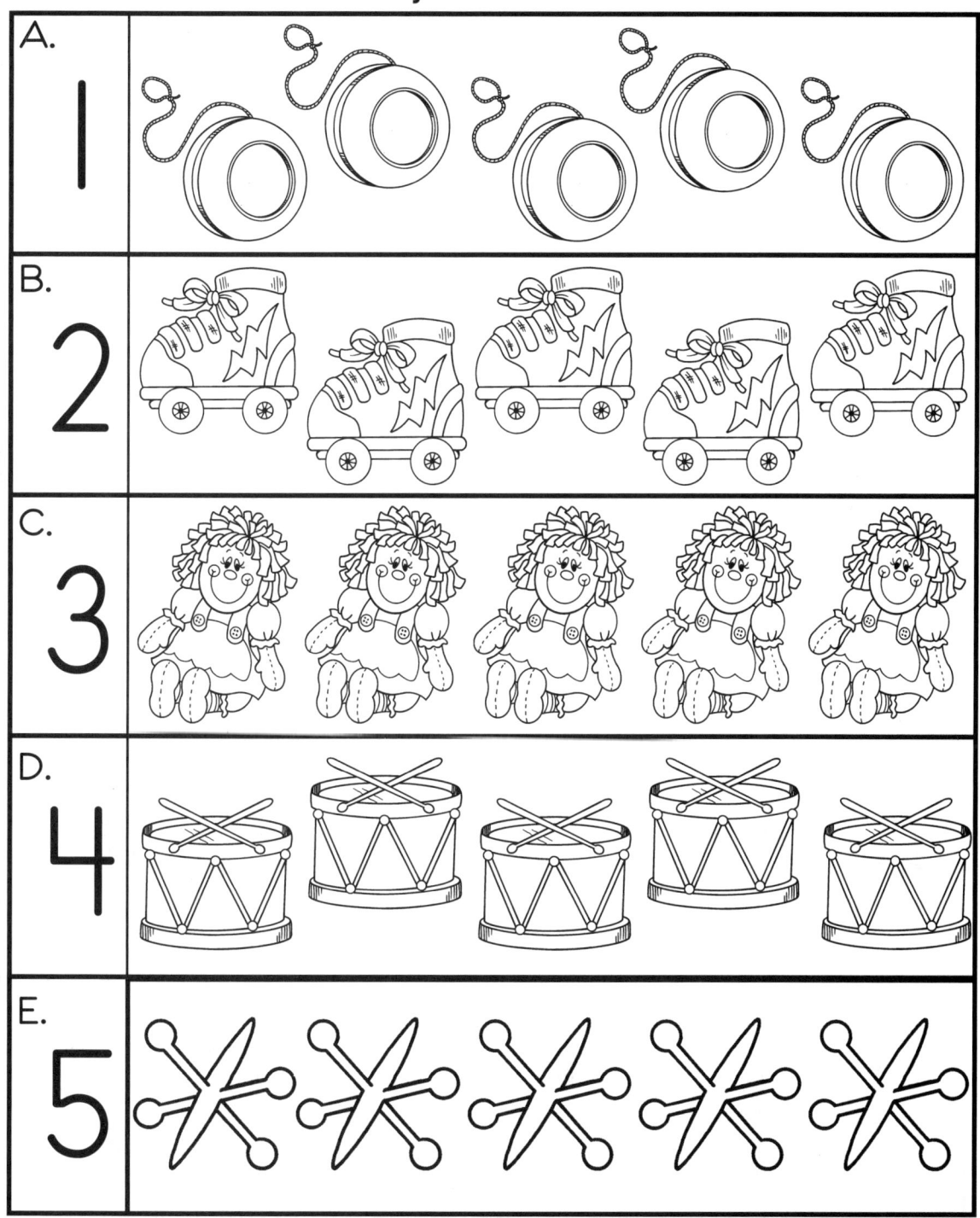

Curriculum Area: Math   **Skills:** Recognizing Numerals, Counting, Fine Motor Skills

Read the **numeral** at the beginning of each row. Put an X on that number of animals in the row.

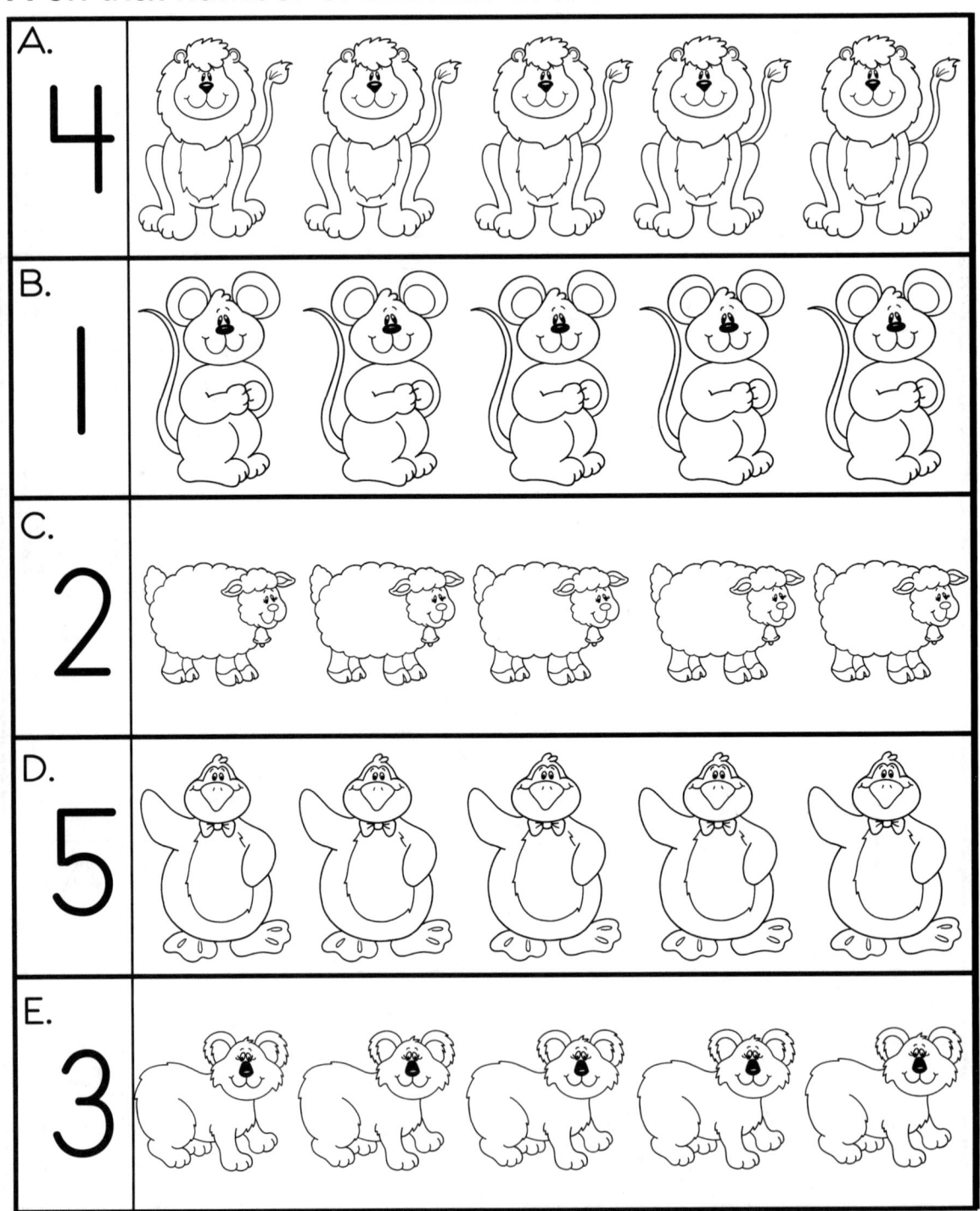

Curriculum Area: Math   **Skills:** Recognizing Numerals, Counting, Fine Motor Skills